You're a Good Sport,

Charlie Brown

Charles M. Schulz

SCHOLASTIC BOOK SERVICES
NEW YORK · TORONTO · LONDON · AUCKLAND · SYDNEY · TOKYO

I appreciate your taking me
to play tennis, Linus.

ISBN: 0-590-08502-6

12 11 10 9 8 7 6 5   9/7 0 1 2/8
            Printed in the U.S.A.

That's the only trouble with tennis. You can't play it alone.

Maybe we won't get to play tennis at all. The courts are all full.

The courts are always full of big kids, and they never let you play.

I hate big kids! They never give you a chance! They play all day.

Just you watch! They'll hog the courts all day! They'll just keep on playing and playing. They'll never. . . .

You big kids get off that court right now,

or my boyfriend will clobber you!

That's the only trouble with tennis.
You can't play it alone.

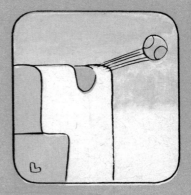

At last Snoopy's going to play a real game!

WAP!

...WOODSTOCK!!!

Hiya, Sal. Glad to see you. I came over to invite Snoop to a great event.

Hey, Snoop! I want to talk to you.

We're having a real Motocross, and I'm recruiting guys like you to enter the race.

It's for charity, and the winner's gonna get a great prize. A good athlete like you just can't turn down such a challenge.

So get yourself a bike,
Snoop old boy, and we'll
see you at the races!

Hi, gang! Let me
give you a flash on
what's new. It's called
Motocross!

MOTOCROSS????

It's the sport that's
sweeping the nation.
And it tells all about it
in this folder.

Instead of a regular race track, the course is made up of jumps, sandbars, rocks, dry riverbeds, wet riverbeds, and whoop-de-dos.

All these obstacles are designed to test the rider's skill. Skill is a lot more important than speed.

And you get to ride a neat bike like this.

The winner gets two tickets to the Pro Bowl game. So get yourselves some bikes and join the fun!

See you at the track!

Hey, that's a good idea, Charlie Brown. You should get a bike and enter the Motocross. I'll be your pit crew.

Me? How will I ever afford a motorbike? I'm not a millionaire.

Look, Charlie Brown, this is a great opportunity for you. If you just go home and empty out your piggy bank, I'm sure you can swing it. And don't forget that I'll be your pit crew.

Okay, crew, how about if we open *our* piggy banks and see if *we* can buy a bike.

Hey, Linus, how about this
one? Or this one? Or. . . .

Do you think it runs?

I hate to tell you this,
Charlie Brown, but this
little bike is all we can afford.

I think we'll be money ahead
even if it walks!

Hey, Chuck, I'm glad you made it. We'll have a great race. I sure hope you can make a decent showing — maybe a fourth or a fifth.

Of course I'll come in first
and get the grand prize!

MOTO CROSS
CONTESTANTS
7. P.PATTY   12. S.CLAXTON
13. C.BROWN 15. J.JONES
1. MASKED
   MARVEL   25. D.RO
   SMITH   56. J.WO
   ILL

Oh, brother!

Hey, Marcie, look at that! Old Chuck Brown is in my heat. And look at this. Some kid calls himself the Masked Marvel.

Boy, this is great! Chuck'll be no problem to me. And this Masked Marvel sounds like a joke.

This is Marcie in the pit area. We're about to interview this contestant. Hi, sir. I see you have an interesting bike there. Care to let the fans in on your strategy?

Come on, kids, let's get to
the bikes and get ready.

Hey, well,
now that. . . .

That's very
interesting.

There you have it, fans, the strategy of Peppermint Patty.

Now let's go on to this interesting biker.

Let's see, you're listed here as the Masked Marvel. Would you like to let the fans know what your strategy is?

Ar. . . .

Isn't that interesting, fans?

Drama,

sheer drama!

Hey, Chuck, here's the guy
to watch for!

The Masked Marvel!

Masked Marvel?

This is big time, Chuck!
The Marvel doesn't go out for
amateur meets, you know!

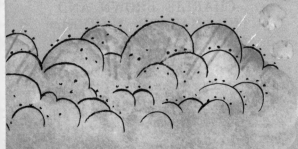

CHARLIE BROWN AND
THE MASKED MARVEL
ARE WIPED OUT!

CHARLIE BROWN HAS
LOST HIS HELMET!

Here comes the ambulance!

The ambulance has picked up Charlie Brown and the Masked Marvel!

Hey, what's this?
They put me at the vet!

The Motocross! I've
got to get back to
the Motocross!

Ah, here's a pumpkin just the right size.

Just don't start pulling any of that Great Pumpkin stuff on me, Linus.

Oh, Charlie Brown. . . .

It's the rule. You've got to wear a helmet. And this fits perfectly!

Good grief!

Hooray! Charlie Brown and the Masked Marvel are back in the race!

Here it is, fans, late in the race. Three of the contestants are far in the lead — the Masked Marvel, Peppermint Patty, and . . . Charlie Brown.

The Masked Marvel is ahead!

Yeah! The Masked Marvel!

It's Charlie Brown! Charlie Brown
is winning the Motocross!

How about that?
Old Charlie Brown
is first! I think the
world is coming to
an end.

You won, Charlie Brown!
You won! You get the prize!

And here is the Motocross Queen to present you with your prize — a gift certificate for five haircuts! We couldn't get the Pro Bowl tickets, kid, so we got you five free haircuts!

Haircuts? But my dad is a barber! And besides, I don't have much hair to cut!

Don't feel too bad, Charlie Brown. Winning the big prize isn't the important thing.

What matters is that you tried your best.

And by doing your best, you beat them all. You came in first, Charlie Brown!

Hey . . . !

Okay, gang, I've got the winning spirit. I've finally got the winning combination. Now that I've won my first race, nothing can stop me.

After 980 straight defeats, we're finally going to win our first baseball game! Take your positions.

I've got the winning
spirit, now. I'll just wind up
and burn it right by this
guy. Here I go. . . .